Soul Prosperity
Your Health & Your Money

Freshwater Press

All Scripture references taken from the KJV of the Holy Bible, unless otherwise indicated.

SOUL PROSPERITY: *Your Health & Your Money*

Book 3 of the **SOUL Prosperity Series**

> The Motherboard: Key to Soul Prosperity
>
> SOUL Captivity
>
> Soul Prosperity: Your Health & Your Money
>
> Fantasy Spirit Spouse
>
> *All by Dr. Marlene Miles*

Freshwater Press USA

ISBN: 978-1-960150-21-9

eBook Version

Copyright 2023, Dr. Marlene Miles

All rights reserved. No part of this book may be reproduced, distributed, or transmitted by any means or in any means including photocopying, recording or other electronic or mechanical methods without prior written permission of the publisher except in the case of brief publications or critical reviews.

Table of Contents

What Is Soul Prosperity? 6
Survival Emotions 10
Fake Survival Mode 13
We Don't Live There 15
Beloved, I Wish 18
Proof of the Prospered Soul 21
Devilish Memory Issues 26
Sin Raging Against 28
the Mind (Soul) 28
Devil Agent, Double Agent 30
Reconcile It 33
Peace 36
Danger! 38
Things & Stuff 40
Remember 44
Be Mature 46
Flesh Tends to Poverty 49
Lust of the Flesh 51
Not Prospering 53
A Soul Can Go Either Way 55
The Spirit of God Leads to Wealth 58
Health 62
Where is Your Money? 65
God Will Show Up 69
Where's Your Money? 72

Prospering	76
Soul-Tied	78
Encourage Yourself in The Lord	81
You're a Role Model	83
Prayer	85
Christian books by this author	87

Beloved, I pray above all things
that you would prosper
and be in health,
even as your soul prospers.
3 John 2

What Is Soul Prosperity?

What is soul prosperity? What is physical prosperity? A thriving body. Spiritual prosperity is a thriving spiritual life. So, soul prosperity is a thriving soul. To live, to grow, to advance, and thrive in all aspects of his being is every man's goal from birth to the end of days.

Our souls may start out small, immature or unprospered, but we should not stay that way. To have a prospered soul it needs to be ministered to and that by the Word of God, and time in the presence of God. Your soul should be ministered to by your spirit man who is receiving from the Spirit of God. The soul will not thrive in an echo chamber when it only talks to itself. The soul has a mind, and it can talk. It can talk to itself, and it also talks to the flesh--, often. But the soul needs more than that to thrive and prosper.

> Wherefore laying aside all malice, and all guile, and hypocrisies, and envies, and all evil speakings,
> As newborn babes, desire the sincere milk of the word, that ye may grow thereby:
> 1 Peter 2:1-2

To *prosper* means to succeed, to flourish, do well, blossom, improve, expand, progress or make progress. It means to get ahead, perhaps move to a *dee*-lux apartment in the sky, to move on up and live one's best life.

Prosper, in the Greek means *to help on the road or succeed in reaching*. Prosperity is more than money, but money is involved. Prosperity includes physical prosperity, financial prosperity and spiritual prosperity as well.

> For I know the plans I have for you, declares the Lord, plans to prosper you and not to harm you, plans to give you hope and a future. Jeremiah 29:11

The Lord definitely wants to prosper us. The verse above doesn't say in *what* way, although most people want more money so most believe God is talking about money. But I believe God intends to prosper us in *all* ways, in every way. Therefore our opening Scripture would prove true as we prosper in our souls, our health *and* money will prosper as well.

All this prospering has to be God's way because the devil constantly offers shortcuts and lays snares for a mankind.

A man can ***appear*** as though he's prospering but he may be in the bowels of hell already, hell on Earth, or on his way to some region of captivity. He could *look* prosperous in one way but be captive to the devil in another aspect of his soul or being. Look at one of my favorite verses:

> I Nebuchadnezzar was at rest in mine house, and flourishing in my palace:
> Daniel 4:4

Nebuchadnezzar was a king. He lived in a palace, and he sincerely believed he had it made. He said he was at rest and flourishing, but was he? Flourishing implies that he is on his way up and not on his way down. We learn from the Book of Daniel that at that time Nebuchadnezzar was on his way **down** in the eyes of God due to Nebuchadnezzar's own behavior.

The lesson for us is that we never want to be at ease when we should not be at ease. We never be arrogant when we should be meek. We never think more highly of ourselves or our situations than we ought. And we never want to do evil to God's anointed and appointed. All those emotions, actions, and behaviors are typical of those who are *unprospered* in their souls.

Beloved I pray above all things that thou mayest prosper and be in health even as thy soul prospers. So we are dealing with the prosperity of one's soul. We want to know how to get to soul prosperity so we can have the other blessings that go along with the verse--, health and wealth. Our souls, which include our mind, will, and intellect can effect and affect our lives dramatically. Mostly we have been and will continue to deal with emotions as we look at the mind aspect of the soul.

Survival Emotions

We discussed in what became the first book of this series, **The Motherboard: Key to Soul Prosperity** that God gives us **memory** for at least one very simple reason: *Man has a tendency to forget.* So God gave us memory to save our lives and keep us alive. In a crisis situation one wrong response can be disastrous, or even deadly. So we need to remember things such as, come in from the storm, especially if there's lightning or heavy rain. A blizzard is really cold and life threatening. A desert has little or no water.

Choosing an emotional response when a spiritual response or an intellectually, well-thought-out response is needed can be ruinous to property and life.

Emotions can take a person into survival mode, *Oh my! It's raining and lightning a lot! What should I do?* What did you do last time? And did it work? Because of memory we have the same or different responses to situations in our lives. God did this to save our lives and keep us alive. We store those memories appropriately in our minds (souls) to retrieve and use later.

But, when memories of crises become stored in or tied to the emotions that can be very powerful, to the negative or positive. When the emotions take over the operation of a person or that person's life, most is put into *survival mode*. Everything is dire, drastic, demanding and right now!

When it comes to a typical baby, survival mode is what all the hollering and crying is about. Until language skills are honed that baby's emotions are running his little life. As far as he knows he may not get food ever again even though he had it two hours ago. The baby's memory is not yet developed enough to know for sure that there will be more food, so his survival emotions kick in.

Like babies, some humans never stop letting their emotions run the show, then parents and other adults are at their mercy their entire childhood--, or their entire lives.

The adult with the vivid memory and what they *believe* was a very hard childhood usually has emotions that have hijacked their entire brain…mind…. soul. Everything is stress and drama, everything is right now, right now, hurry up and everything is worry, worry, what if, *what if!* If not careful this type person will get a bazooka weapon to fire at an ant because he is in full survival mode.

A person with survival mode emotions may kill to avoid being killed even when there is no threat of danger. Survival emotions are not prospered emotions.

Beloved, I pray above all things that you would prosper and be in health *even* as your soul prospers. Nope. Neither health nor wealth, outside of hook and crook, will be in the life of the unprospered soul, according to 3 John 2.

Fake Survival Mode

Saved folk are supposed to be different, because we are new creations in Christ, we are new people. We have renewed minds. We do not act as the world does. We *respond* to things with the information we receive, and already have onboard, but we don't do what the unprospered do.

We purpose to stay out of survival mode because for one thing, no person, no soul ***prospers*** in survival mode. They may <u>maintain</u>, they may get by, *but they will **<u>not</u>** prosper*. If you see a person in survival mode but they <u>**are**</u> prospering, they are faking something. They are either faking the prosperity or they are faking and are only pretending to be in survival mode.

Countless times I've either seen or heard of souls who are needy, needy, needy, and are hitting everyone up for money, help, and goods. It's a shake down. They *appear* to be in survival mode, but they are not. I know a woman who was suffering so much, according to her. Yet, her nails had a regular $100. manicure, her clothes were strictly designer, she drove a late model imported car, not the wind-up kind, but a full-size nice, foreign car, and she lived in a beautiful home. But to hear her say what she was going through you would believe that woman was barely making it.

I often think of the nice people who got together and bought her a new, full-sized (domestic, not imported) refrigerator because she didn't know what she was going to do about her food situation. The refrigerator in her home was broken and she needed fresh food. The new appliance was delivered while she was on vacation in *Paris*.

Don't be duped, unless you want to be.

We Don't Live There

The fact that a person was afflicted, felt threatened, was assaulted and got out of a plight, well Hallelujah! But, without God, an imprint is left on their mind and in their memory. Without a God-focus, their flesh may have gotten out of a problem, *but their emotions, their soul still remembers the problem and it is stamped as UNHEALED, Unfinished--,* or *This Could Happen Again.*

For our benefit God gives us memory to keep us alive.

To our chagrin, memories, wrongly learned, wrongly stored, and called up erroneously can be to our detriment.

If we have gone through a hard time or very difficult event, this is when we need God to restore our souls; put us back to factory settings, or better, so we can live by faith, not in or by fear, as the *Just* should.

Without God, there is still a flesh memory, a residual worry. So, if a similar situation presents, a man may behave the same way, or worse if he thinks he didn't respond strongly enough the first time.

For example, a person who may have been mugged or attacked may have safely gotten away from an attacker. They may have gotten their purse or wallet back and the attacker never took their valuables, or ever learned where they live. But now when the near-victim walks down the street, day or night, they walk circumspectly. Their head turns like a tennis match referee, left to right, to left, expecting *sudden* evil.

They may not even feel secure at home, jumping every time they feel that someone is behind them, when they don't hear footsteps when a family member is approaching their vicinity. That is not a prospered soul.

A prospered soul knows that and because of God, they sleep, they dwell in safety. They know the Lord is their Protector and they dwell under the Shadow of the Almighty. They do not fear what lurks in the shadow of the Valley of Death, no matter what has happened in the past. Even though they've been *through* their souls are **restored** to live normally again. They do not let their Memory hijack their soul and run it with emotions, especially fear-based survival emotions.

To heal that broken or wounded soul, we think we know what attribute God should have showed up in. God is not slack. Are you one of His and did you pray? **Then He showed up.** Did you meet Him? Did you open the door for Him as He stood there and knocked? Did you accept *visitation* from the Lord?

If so, God saved you from the attack and also healed and *restored* your soul. **A restored soul is a prospered soul.**

Your flesh may be strong and bulky and maybe you can fight off an attacker, but **you cannot restore your own soul**. As long as you rely on your own flesh, over God, you've set up your flesh as an idol, as your protector. The flesh will always want to take over because the flesh trusts nothing and no one. The flesh is not even trustworthy itself, so what are we talking about here?

> And I know that nothing good lives in me, that is, in my sinful nature. I want to do what is right, but I can't. Romans 7:18

Beloved, I Wish

Beloved, *I pray above all things that you would be in health and prosper even as your soul prospers*. That verse is a mandate for **us** to prosper our souls, even if we start out small, we grow from faith to faith and from strength to strength.

Coupling 1 Thessalonians 5:23 with 1 Thessalonians 4:4 that we are told to possess our souls and present our souls blameless before the Lord. **We** have to do it ourselves; we have to prosper our *own* souls. No one can do it for us. Our parents try when they teach us to behave ourselves, treat others well, and not hold on to past hurts. The grade schoolteacher attempts to impart it to us by teaching the Golden Rule. The Sunday School teacher does their part with Bible lessons and *Veggie Tales* videos. Many of the disciplines of childhood and life in general are disciplines for the soul, that is the emotions, the will, and the intellect, but especially the emotions.

I've never once heard it said that a man's intellect hijacked his soul, and it was a disaster. (Although a person can *overthink* a matter.) A stubborn man's *will* can cause problems for him, but foremost the **emotions** can mutiny, and overtake the logical mind and become the villain by leading a man astray or into danger.

It is ultimately up to *us* if we grow up or not. Yes, we should grow up and become mature saints, and not stay baby saints needing the sincere milk of the Word only, all of our lives. We are admonished about having to be taught all over again when we, ourselves should be teaching others.

The Word says that we should acknowledge God to direct our paths and not lean on our own understanding. Human understanding is mostly built on *feel like it* or *don't feel like it*. It's built on *I want,* or *I don't want, and* too often it is built on memory, mostly *what **happened** last time*.

In the book, ***Souls in Captivity*** we discussed several types of memory, because in a carnal man, human decisions are, too many times, based on flesh memory, human intellect and especially **<u>emotions</u>**.

Human action, especially if a reaction or a quick response is needed most often is based on muscle memory, or on emotions, especially *survival emotions*. The problem is that survival emotions are **not** prosperity emotions.

Proof of the Prospered Soul

God said it is the main reason why we need soul prosperity. Another reason is one-another ministry; to get along with other saints we need prospered souls.

To get along with sinners we need soul prosperity. You put two sinners together, there may be tension–, not always--, if they both agree to walk together in their sin, they'll get along, at least for a season. Saved or unsaved, you get two unprospered souls together there will be tension and probably fights. This could be why family holidays among unprospered souls can be so traumatic.

The sinner doesn't have a prospered soul. So now imagine two or more sinners at loggerheads over that parking space in front of the large retail chain store. There are 200 parking spaces out there, but they each want ***that one***. They each need to be in front of the store and not have to walk an extra 10 steps.

Hot-heads, and hot-tempered people do not have soul prosperity. Their emotions are in survival mode and that's a very stressful place to live. That's an unprospered soul, the very opposite a prospered soul. Cool, calm, and collected is descriptive of a prospered soul in an emergency situation.

Jesus said: **Agree with your adversary quickly**, this was one lesson on how to get along with people. A prospered soul gets along with others. Agree with your adversary quickly, but not to the point of being killed if it is a **real** life or death situation. Discern every *spirit*.

In the Old Testament, Moses' Levitical Law was outside of man; it was a *what to do* teaching. Jesus's instruction to us is **how to BE, the Spirit of God is in us, and He teaches us** *how to be. Being* surpasses doing any day.

A beautiful example of being and how to ***be*** is found in the Beatitudes of the Sermon on the Mount. We will discuss portions of it as **proof** of soul prosperity. Here are some ways we can know if we have a prospered soul, if we are prospering in our souls based on this portion of Scripture.

- Blessed are the poor in spirit: for theirs is the kingdom of heaven (Matt 5:3).

God blesses those who realize that they are *poor* in Spirit because they seek Him. Their spirit man is not built up and they recognize that. People who are weak in spirit have no heart, no courage, no stick-to-it-ness. Receiving the Kingdom of Heaven is not only getting riches, it *is getting true riches.* Looking at 3 John 2 we can see that being in health and prospering even as our soul prospers shows that being given the Kingdom of Heaven PROVES a prospered soul, else God wouldn't do it.

Jesus also said, **"Marvel not that the demons are subject to you, but *that* your name is written in the Lamb's Book of Life."** A prospered soul will not marvel *that* he *received* the **Kingdom of Heaven** because his soul was already matured, and ready to receive it. He was able to receive it, he had capacity to receive it. A prospered soul realizes the magnitude, the gravity, and the responsibility of receiving it. Responsibility is attached to everything you get from God. You will have to give account as to how you used it and what you did with it.

Gifts of God are not disposable. The wise, prospered, sober soul knows that gifts from God cannot go to your head. Prospered souls don't let things go to their head because their souls are <u>not</u> running their lives.

Like you, with your kids, family, or friends, God does not like it when He gives us things that go to our head. The "head" part of our soul is the *self, id, or ego*. It's a shame when the **head** of anyone is their ego; the Head should be God. When the head is the ego, that in itself is a sign of an unprospered, narcissistic soul.

- Blessed are they that mourn: for they shall be comforted (Matthew 5:4).

A prospered soul has compassion for others. Being comforted and being able to receive comfort is not only a sign of a prospered soul, but it is also **health** to our bones, health to both the soul and body. Comfort may be for physical ailments, or it may be for the emotions--, or both.

- Blessed are the meek: for they shall inherit the earth (Matthew 5:5).

1 Corinthians 13, the Love Chapter shows us the picture of prospered souls. Not only do most of the Spiritual gifts work by Love, but walking in *agape* Love is also the sign of a matured soul in the Lord.

- Blessed are the pure in heart: for they shall see God (Matthew 5:8).

God is patient, and Jesus said to allow the little children to come unto Him, but do you think He wants a bunch of unprospered souls running around Heaven? That could have been the problem when that war broke out in Heaven, (Revelations 12:7). We all love babies and children, but every day, all day?

God brings health, wealth, and in His presence fullness of joy, peace and all the Fruit of the Spirit. Again, proof of the soul's prosperity.

- Blessed are the peacemakers: for they shall be called the children of God (Matthew 5:9).

Being a child of God means you are fully adopted. It is more proof of the prospered soul, that's a blessing, again--, true riches. God deals in the best. He will give the full promises in the fulness of time; when people are mature or maturing.

We need soul prosperity to have the right reactions, and responses. To get out of survival mode, to stay out of captivity, to not take regrettable, inappropriate, drastic actions in life we need prospered souls. We need a right spirit, a good heart and souls that are more like Christ.

Devilish Memory Issues

God gives us **memory** for our good; not to torment us. The devil misuses memory, if he can, to get into our minds, to torment and worry folk. God gave us memory. It's a good thing. But the devil uses it to cause us to remember things that we <u>**don't**</u> need to remember. The devil is famous for playing and replaying mistakes, errors, and missteps over and over in your mind to bring torment.

As he brings you things you don't need to remember, it can cause a man to become or remain upset or worried and then hinder his own soul's prosperity.

Everything has memory. You can probably remember the sounds and smells of Christmas in your momma's or your grandmother's house.

God gave us memory because He's so good to us, He has nothing to hide so He gave us *evolved memory* so we could remember Him and learn progressively.

Conversely, Satan also sneaks, hides, and *takes* memory so we don't recall what he has done to us. What do I mean? The devil encourages drugs and drinking, so we can do things that are not godly and then *forget* what we did, forget the problems we encountered and in so doing be tricked into inebriation again.

Worse, the devil wants us to forget what *he* did to us while we were in rebellion, incapacitated, or in ignorance. Not the scope of this book, but there are dream snatchers, night raiders who cover our dreams to make us forget what we dreamed so we won't remember what we did in the dream, what the devil and other players *did to us* in the dream, or what we may have **agreed** to in the dream. In the latter, that's how some evil covenants are ratified – while you are asleep--, in the dream. Told you he was sneaky; he's not just evil, the devil is tricky enough to *take away* memory. Proving that he is the opposite of God.

Sin Raging Against the Mind (Soul)

Another thing that works against soul prosperity is sin, especially lust, but really any kind of sin. The soul is capable of lust (Deuteronomy 12:20); it wants what it wants. It wants what it had yesterday, it wants the leeks and garlic of Egypt. Please tell me that no soul would be willing to go **back** into captivity for some cucumbers and garlic.

The soul is dangerous, I hope you are finding this out, so you know to trust your spirit man and not the flesh and not your soul unless the soul is prospered in the Lord.

> But I see another law at work in me, waging war against the law of my mind and making me a prisoner of the law of sin at work within me.
>
> Romans 7:23 NIV

A prospered soul has reached perfection. That perfection is LOVE, *agape*. An unprospered soul, and unprospered heart is childish and immature and usually selfishly gives in to sin and temptations.

But the soul that is prospering or is fully prospered has a resistance to temptations and the wiles of the devil. Yes, because he may know the tactics of the devil, but also the mature soul is not starving or even hungry for flesh experiences, *things, or stuff*.

God is LOVE. Jesus is LOVE when we attune our souls to our spirits which are attuned to the Spirit of God that is LOVE.

Afflicting one's flesh in a <u>Godly</u> fast is how the flesh is kept *under* and it is also how the soul grows and matures. Like a spoiled child if you give your flesh and/or soul everything it wants and everything it asks for or demands you will have very undisciplined flesh and a runaway soul that could land you in captivity, in hell.

Devil Agent, Double Agent

Soul prosperity is needed to **resist** the devil and his advances, because a **person who is not prospered in their soul can easily become an agent of Satan**.

What?

Yup, I said that.

An unprospered soul wants revenge and payback. They are easily hurt and stay hurt. *Perceived* wrongs send them into a tizzy. Unmet needs make them feel entitled, offended and wounded. Seeing others with things that they, themselves want or feel they deserve makes them resentful and jealous. All of these works of the flesh are counterproductive against a prospered soul.

We need prospered souls so we can be in health and prosper in all the other areas of life --, *even* as our souls prosper.

The Lord's prayer states, *"Forgive us our debts AS we forgive our debtors."* There is a requirement to the Lord forgiving us. Even AS your soul prospers assumes that the thesis will happen if the premise does.

The flesh wants to take OVER to the exclusion of letting the soul or parts of the soul have a voice, and the flesh most assuredly does not want the spirit to take over. The spirit of man is led by the Spirit of God; the dictates of the Spirit of God are too regimented for the immature soul and especially for the flesh. The prospered soul rejoices in the discipline and security of the Spirit of God.

The flesh wants to eat, drink, party, live it up and sleep. Then it wants to do it again. The soul wants to run things by how it *feels*, emotionally, or intellectually and it wants its way. A man's **will** is seated in the soul of that man making him flexible or stubborn.

You can pretty much guess outcomes of a person's life based on whether their flesh, soul or spirit is running their life.

Here's the stuff the flesh wants to do:

When you follow the desires of your sinful nature, the results are very clear: sexual immorality, impurity, lustful pleasures, idolatry, sorcery, hostility, quarreling, jealousy, outbursts of anger, selfish ambition, dissension, division, envy, drunkenness, wild parties, and other sins like these. Let me tell you again, as I have before, that anyone living that sort of life will not inherit the Kingdom of God. (Galatians 5:19-21)

Untamed, unsaved flesh will do those things whenever it can and because it can, because the heart of man is deceitfully wicked.

Reconcile It

Getting one's soul to prosper, or at least stopping it from **not** prospering is the challenge. We are to possess our souls and present them, blameless to the Lord at the appropriate time.

A man in the Earth has a flesh body, does he even think about his *soul*? Mostly man walks by sight and what he sees is flesh, and other flesh--, his and other people's--, that he may or may not be attracted to. Mating seems to be a big part of the picture for most humans.

So, this flesh body allows him to do physical things in the Earth. He also has a soul, which he cannot see, and he is a spirit which he also cannot see. Man has to make an *effort* to work on the invisible things in his life while his flesh, that he can see, and *feel*, wants to take dominance, loom large and be the center of attention – always. The flesh demands to be fed three or more times a day. The flesh wants to be doing something all the time. It craves, lusts, wants, and demands things that can get a man in trouble, captivity, or send him straight to hell.

What does the soul ask for? The unprospered soul wants emotional needs met for the most part. It knows an eye for an eye and a tooth for a tooth. Whatever it goes through or *feels*, if it's negative it wants to give that back. If it's positive, it probably thinks, *Great, I'm wonderful so I deserved that, I'm not giving anything back.*

What type of feeding does your spirit request? It should hunger and thirst after the Word, after God, and God's presence, ideally.

The soul has intellect, but it needs management. In proper alignment, **your spirit man manages the soul.**

The three realms: the flesh, the soul, and spirit don't necessarily work together, but they need to work harmoniously. If the flesh takes the lead, the soul and the spirit will suffer. If the soul takes the lead, the flesh will be kept in check, or as it states in the KJV, the flesh will be kept *under*.

War within our members until we decide or let the Spirit of God decide who will run our daily life. The wise man will choose the Holy Spirit to direct man's spirit man. That is where success and the peace lie.

> For he himself is our peace, who has made the two groups one and has destroyed the barrier, the dividing wall of hostility,
>
> by setting aside in his flesh the law with its commands and regulations. His purpose was to create in himself one new humanity out of the two, thus making peace,
>
> and in one body to reconcile both of them to God through the cross, by which he put to death their hostility.
>
> He came and preached peace to you who were far away and peace to those who were near.
>
> Ephesians 2:14-17 NIV

The ideal is for the spirit man to take the lead in running a man's life because the spirit is the most trustworthy and balanced referee of the three parts of the triune man.

Peace

You keep him in perfect peace whose mind is stayed
on you, because he trusts in you.
Isaiah 26:3 ESV

Peace draws prosperity. War repels it.

Peace fosters health in the human body. War promotes fear, stress and emotional upheaval which all can lead to disease, somatic symptoms, syndromes and of course, death.

Peace, when present is the proof that right choices have been made, good decisions have been made and the soul is not in survival mode but is able to prosper.

Where there is war, the enemies of God are there so God is not dropping off provisions for your enemies to get or to take from you, but He does prepare a table in the *presence* of your enemies. Jesus was at a table in the presence of Judas. The prosperous soul ushers in peace and fosters peace, the unprosperous causes a ruckus most of the time. Prosperity and health travel with peace.

There is such a peace that comes with the God-focus that it can heal other parts of your life. The ruckus caused by the soul and flesh jockeying for opposition has to be settled and reconciled. That is accomplished by the Spirit of God having ministered to the spirit of man who is leading a man.

Danger!

An unprospered soul is dangerous, especially when it is in fear, hatred, jealousy, or survival mode and they find ways to express their fear and other emotions and modes.

If they express it physically, they hurt others, physically.

If they express it soulishly, they hurt others emotionally, in their emotions--, hurt feelings, wounded souls and the like.

If they express it spiritually, they really hurt others, depending on what spirit(s) was invoked to create a certain spiritual outcome. Many spiritual actions cannot be undone or stopped by simply stopping the behavior. Oftentimes a cascade of events is set in motion that takes a great deal of prayer, fasting, and deliverance to stop.

An unprospered soul is greedy. Hungry. Tempt-able. Bribe-able. It thinks it is in survival mode, which makes the unprospered soul *desperate*. That soul may think it's in a life-or-death situation 24/7, or often, when it really isn't. That rumbling outside is not mortars dropping from across the border; it's just thunder.

(PTSD is a survival mode and the person with it needs healing so they can enjoy a victorious life. This book is not to pass judgment on anyone, especially those who have seen war THANK YOU for your Service!) This book is about the average everybody who grew up the average way, but the challenges of life may have visited their house too often, too strongly or left them fragmented, broken or possibly spiritually captive without even knowing it – and how to get out of that trouble.)

An unprospered soul **sins** and may become a devil agent, condemning their soul by the cascade of events that begins as they start the revenge, get-even, payback, or kill-or-be-killed reaction.

An unprospered soul is bound. It is tied to the memories that tell it that it is in survival mode, and it must react strongly, when it really isn't. An unprospered soul in an adult is not just bound, it is often hell bound.

Things & Stuff

When unprospered souls want something, they may scorch the Earth to get it--, by any means necessary. Once they attain the thing that they desperately want, they will fight and struggle--, most often they **have** to fight and struggle all their lives to **keep** anything that they've "acquired" by unscrupulous methods.

With Soul Prosperity when you receive the things you're supposed to receive, you <u>get to **keep** them</u>. You receive them from God, or *through people* by the Spirit of God. You get to keep them because God *gave* them to you.

> The blessings of the Lord maketh rich and He adds no sorrow with it. Proverbs 10:22

How do you behave when you don't have the things you want, desire and *feel* you really deserve, shows whether your soul is prospering. If your soul is not prospering, **when (*if*)** you receive those things, you may become over protective of those things guarding them religiously, to keep them. Without God, perhaps you were never to get those things because they may harm you, or worse, you may harm other people with those things.

A husband-and-wife team worked hard for years to grow a business. They reach their goal of being worth a million dollars. The husband suddenly changed from being a husband, reverting to being only a *man*. He left his wife to pursue women out in the streets. His soul was not prospered; he got what he wanted and reverted to putting his flesh back in charge. (A person can *act* but for so long.)

Women, let me warn you that you cannot **make** a man's soul prosper. No one can, only God and by that man's permission, and his submission to the Holy Spirit. Neither can a woman's soul be ***made*** to prosper. If she is hell bent on "making a man over" she might go through hell and never accomplish that goal. If she wants the image-driven life where she *appears* to have a husband and *appears* to be married, that can be arranged. All you need is another unprospered soul who can be bribed, tempted or bought. He will go along with that as long as there is something in it for him. *But what is that devil-made relationship, really?*

Men and women of God who become fathers and mothers, you can show your children, teach your children, discipline your children, and it is your job. But whether their soul prospers or not is told in their teen years if they are just going along to get along, or if they are really transforming into adulthood and acquiring the Mind of Christ. It will definitely be seen in their 20's as soon as they leave the house and can *"do as they please."*

Parents and all other "grown" people, God is looking at us like that too.

God gave us our memory to keep our minds stayed on Him and you believe that you are. You may ask, *"God, in my natural life, why am I going **through**? Why am I going through this? Why am I going through that? Why am I...? Why is all this happening to me all the time?"*

When Jesus was tempted of the devil, He was tempted with *things and stuff*. Jesus made right, God-focused decisions. Jesus had God on His mind, and even more than that, Jesus had **you** on His mind, He had me on His mind, Hallelujah!

After resisting temptation, look where Jesus is now. He has it all. The world is His footstool. He is the King of kings. He received everything that He was going to get anyway, without caving into devil temptations. Jesus received it all with His soul intact and **_with soul prosperity._**

Could that be why you are going through? Repeating the same tests and temptations over and over until you pass them?

Remember

Memory – internal memory, it's so you have a ready reminder of God, what He did for you, how He blessed you--, even a reminder of what He is doing for you right now. A God-focused memory will create a prospered soul. When you remember God as your Healer, your Provider, your Protector. Amen.

Soul prosperity keeps you from doing stupid things. It helps you to not sin. It helps you to resist temptations. When your spirit is led by God's Spirt and you train your soul to submit to your spirit man instead of to itself (emotions) or your flesh man, that's soul prosperity. Ultimately, when your soul is submitting to the Spirit of God, (via your own spirit man), that's soul prosperity.

You have a reminder *in* your soul, it's called memory. That memory is inside you, internally, on your own *motherboard* of how God is your provider, and then you have a reminder of how God will never forsake you or leave you.

You have a natural reminder, something you went through. It's a time of day, a place, a date, and you remember. That's the memorial.

In the Old Testament the Spirit of God was on the outside, its why God had OT men build memorials. The way we learn and that we learn and how we pass on our family and people's history, and teach our children and children's children, was by external memorials in the olden days. Now we have the Holy Spirit. So everything was outside of them. We have the Better Covenant, the Better Blood and the Holy Spirit, so thank You, Jesus. Everything's inside, so our memorials, are on the inside so we can remember Him, keep our mind, *stayed* on Him.

This internal memory is to keep our minds stayed on God until we actually *get it*. We keep going through stuff, until we SEE God. And keeping a God-focused memory prospers our souls.

Order my steps in thy word: and let not any iniquity have dominion over me.
Psalms 119:133

Be Mature

Here comes an immature, childish, ungodly thought or impulse – internal Motherboard, what do you say? Have you seen this before, and how do I handle it?

The motherboard, your **internal processor** needs to be applied to this possibly random thought to either raise it up, elevate it, mother it to godliness, or cast it out immediately.

Soul prosperity is a RESISTANCE against an evil enemy bent on captivity, destruction, death, stealing, or killing. Who do you think is giving you those ideas to scorch the Earth and annihilate your brothers and sisters, in Christ?

The unprospered soul gives into the temptation to think of himself, *his* wants, *his* needs, *his* goals in life. How he can get those things, how much he can get and how soon he can get as much as he can. Temptation, the likes that Jesus experienced in the Wilderness by Satan will come. Offers such as, *I will give you this, that and the other if you will bow down to me* will come. The unprospered soul will most often fail those temptations.

Who's tempting that unprospered soul? The devil himself? Maybe, maybe not. It could be one of the devil's representatives such as Greed, Pride, Narcissism, Insecurity, or Lust. Of course, anyone who bows down to any of those demons will be on the hook. That opens the door for the next demon, and the next one, and the next. When a soul is not prospered, when it's immature, the wrong choice is often made, and disaster follows.

The devil works with *familiar* and *monitoring spirits*. Those *spirits* are with you as soon as you're born, or shortly after. They are familiar with you and with those in your family line; they've been studying your people for generations. So here comes a temptation, and it's something you like because it would not be a temptation if you didn't like it. It knows what you look at on TV, movies, magazines, it knows what strikes your fancy and presents that to you. Often.

Now when this happens, don't think you are living some charmed life where all the things you like just show up *for* you. **These are tests and temptations**. These things are showing up in the same way as what you look at online suddenly pops up on your screen when you are doing something else completely. Please don't think this is a *confirmation* that you should buy what's being advertised. You're being online-stalked, digitally stalked. Sellers want your money, they want to sell you stuff. It's the same thing, basically as a *familiar spirit*.

Don't forget God. Your internal motherboard, your memory, the memorials **of GOD** in your mind are what remind you of who God is, how He's kept you, and when you know who you are, and you don't bow to demons.

A proper, God-focused *Motherboard* won't let you forget your relationship with God. Have a prospered soul; be mature.

Read my book, **The Motherboard: Key to Soul Prosperity**, for more on this. https://a.co/d/5AD9PLT

Flesh Tends to Poverty

If you're not operating in soul prosperity, you may only be interested in your flesh comforts. Flesh is temporal. Flesh stores up **zero** treasure in Heaven. (Read my book *got Money?)* The image-driven life, the one that carnal-minded people are always concerned with, is all about how to they *look*. How they really <u>*are*</u> is not even on their radar. It's all about appearances and how they *look*. Not only does this person spend a great deal of time and money on their appearance they give little time to Kingdom work, which is what will really prosper their soul.

I know that every time I've gone on a missions trip and I have the audacity to think that I'm there to give, which I am, right? But every time *I* end up changed, improved and bettered by the very people I went to minister to. It's a wonder.

When doing Kingdom work, God is repaying in ***prosperity***. Prosperity of soul is as valuable or more valuable than financial prosperity because prosperity of soul translates to all other kinds of prosperity as we read in 3 John 2: *Beloved, I pray above all things that you would prosper and be in health even as your soul prospers.*

The order of things in the Earth is: Flesh. Soul, and then the spirit of a man, unless a man ***wills*** himself and by the Spirit of God to upset that hierarchy. If he does not upset that natural order, that man will always default to flesh. If you default to flesh first, then the flesh will take over. There will be shopping. There will be hair salons and barbershop visits, and weekly mani-pedi's. There will be gym memberships, possibly plastic surgery, spas, med spas, new cars, big houses, fabulous trips, expensive food, wine and jewelry. This is all temporary stuff that will **burn** in the end, when tried with Fire.

In that set up, the soul: the ***will*** never had a chance. No will power is needed or used to constantly shop. The intellect may be used to calculate the best price on things, but mostly it is the emotions that are soothed by retail therapy--, that is, until the credit card bills come.

Lust of the Flesh

> Dearly beloved, I beseech *you* as strangers and pilgrims, **abstain from fleshly lusts, which war against the soul;**
> Having your conversation honest among the Gentiles that, whereas they speak against you as evildoers, they may by your good works which they shall behold, glorify God in the day of visitation.
> 1 Peter 2:11-12
> *(emphasis added, mine)*

The shopping sprees, the dining extravaganzas, and vacations all feed the lust of the flesh. As stated before, anything that builds up the flesh will do so to the detriment of the spirit man. The flesh wants to be in charge and will exert its influence to take over whenever it is given a chance. That is why we fast to keep our body (flesh) in submission to the Spirit. As also stated before, the flesh and soul war for power and the position of authority in a man's life.

Lusts may come, but giving into the lusts of the flesh will hinder soul prosperity in a big way. Recall, according to 3 John 2, our health and wealth are tied to a prospered soul.

Lust comes and sometimes is presented to us as fantasy. I will mention here and cannot overstress that fantasy, which we may call imagination as children, and we are taught that it is okay or even encouraged can be *very dangerous* when taken too far in children or as adults. It can be extremely dangerous when added to grown up activities, namely, **sex**. Man is ever enticed to sexual sins by the *spirit of lust* and other evil *spirits*.

As I was writing this book, this chapter became an entire book all unto itself and you can find it in my catalog of books, **Fantasy Spirit Spouse.** https://a.co/d/cqIW6H3 I recommend you read it if you have interest in or need to know more about *spirit spouses* in general, and *fantasy spirit spouse* in particular.

Not Prospering

When your soul is not prospering nothing around you or about you will be prospering, not your health and not your money. The opposite of prospering would be to crash, fail, or collapse. Especially when it comes to souls, who wants a tied, fragmented, crushed, or weak soul?

Memorials are built to celebrate victories. Successes are memorialized. Even today, some types of memorials are outside, at the park, in the center of the roundabout, or sometimes they are entire buildings. But memorials are also **inside** of us, in our MEMORY as we have discussed.

Normal people do not build memorials to remember something bad. We have pictures of our mothers, for example, in our homes because our mothers were good to us. Pictures of Mom are not up to remind us of how our mothers made us eat liver and onions or green peas while growing up.

If your mental focus is not right, if your focus is not on good, if it's not *on* God, opportunities to build up your soul will be missed. Consequently, when the need to respond, or to react for yourself, or Minister to others, you could make unprospered soul decisions that could hurt people or drive them away. You, me, any of us could drive people away if we do such things. Some of those people are the ones God has put in place to pray for us and bless us! Some who push people away push their blessings away. Unprospered souls push people away.

God gives us houses, and nice cars. He gives us times of comfort, times of peace where we are free of the worry of war, destruction, or people coming at us with clubs to hit us over the head, as cavemen may have suffered. When we are free from war and the worry of sudden terror, we can prosper our souls.

When we are **out** of survival mode, it is not to brag about how much we have, how nice our house is, how we got ourselves out of harm's way. It's not about the *things and the stuff* or our own heroics; it's about God. It's for soul prosperity. The *things* and the *stuff* are added bonuses.

A Soul Can Go Either Way

If you are always thinking of what another person, whether a pew member, or co-worker did to you, as negative as it is, that person becomes your *idol*. It doesn't matter *why* you think about this thing, event, or person, it is simply THAT you are thinking of them, putting them in front of God that makes them an idol. You can love an idol or hate an idol, just don't think on them more than you think on God.

Doing so, does not demonstrate a renewed mind. That's not a prospering soul. Every time you think about an event that happened to you, positive or negative it lends itself to idolatry. Don't do that.

Even when you think of yourself, every time you think of your house, your car, and your clothes, you think about how **you** did this, how **you** put yourself through university and how you have this great job, and that's still idolatry, that is not soul prosperity.

This is why you have a *motherboard*. That's why you have imprints inside of you, and a **memory** to keep your mind stayed on God, you have a *motherboard* on board. Keep your mind stayed on God.

God is not linear, and He's not so simple that He can just show you one attribute, and that's God. Surely He will show you one attribute at a time, but that is not all there is. God is so awesome and infinite. He wants to manifest Himself to you. And He does that incrementally, sequentially by His attributes and character, He does that by walking with you, and by keeping you, blessing you, and even by giving you the desires of your heart.

No one alive can experience all of God all at once. Each time He does something for you, you should register a reminder of it. *I remember the time that God, and the time **that God**, I remember the time that* God…

If your focus is not on God, you'll remember the times that *you* did something great, or when somebody did such and such *to* you, *for* you, or against you.

God is not a quick study where you think you completely know Him now because you walked down to the altar last Sunday at church.

You can't just get saved, join church, or whatever you call it, and then go back out into the world and party until it's time for Heaven.

It doesn't work like that.

The Spirit of God Leads to Wealth

Depending on how your memory is focused determines how you will respond to life's challenges. If it's God-focused, then your soul is prospering. When your soul prospers, you'll be in health, and prosper financially as well. To get the health and wealth blessings of 3 John 2 we need a well-ordered, prospered soul that God would be well-pleased to see. Maybe God would even be impressed…

From that we infer that keeping your mind focused on evil, on the devil, on hurts, pains and wrongs done to you, you will NOT be in health, but the opposite of health: sickness, disease, disorder will have a place in your life. We can also infer that your finances will suffer.

For I know the plans I have for you," declares the Lord, "**plans to prosper you and not to harm you, plans to give you hope and a future.**

> Then you will call on me and come and pray to me,
> and I will listen to you.
> You will seek me and find me when you seek me with
> all your heart.
> Jeremiah 29:11-13

The tone of your soul, such as your mood does not tell if it is prospering or not. You're born with a certain temperament, so that doesn't tell us if it is prospering, or not. The quiet soul may prosper quietly, or it may suffer and wane to nothing and who would ever know if that person doesn't open their mouth and say something? There is a silent soul that suffers quietly in their room, in their home, in the recesses of their mind. They rehearse wrongs done, hurts, trespasses, unmet needs and disappointments. This type of soul can make a man ill, as well.

If he's too distraught to go to work, or start that business, he will also tend to poverty.

We learned from the Beatitudes, however, that meekness and gentleness of spirit are positive traits in soul prosperity.

Then there is the loud soul who if not prospered tends to rage and anger. He has emotional outbursts. Peter was very defensive of Jesus and cut off the ear of the soldier who was trying to apprehend Jesus in the Garden of Gethsemane when He was betrayed.

John the Baptist, whom I secretly **LOVE** was *"one crying out in the Wilderness."* I'd say JtB was pretty vocal. The loud soul is vocal and not only can do much good in the Kingdom when his soul is sober and mature, but when it's not he can work up a single listener or a whole crowd. The loud soul can work himself up as well. It is not always the case, but you may see high blood pressure and diseases and disorders that go along with that in the boisterous, soul if it is unporospered.

This shows that that unprospered soul will miss the health blessings of 3 John 2.

Unforgiveness can be found in a loud soul or a silent soul but in either, it lends itself to kidney issues. The stubborn, unforgiving man may suffer with neck issues.

Loud, or quiet we should show our moderation, and show ourselves approved. Study to be quiet while at the same time come boldly to the Throne of Grace. This takes God. This takes the Spirit of God to minister to each of us where we are and bring us **balance** so we can be our best, and so we can be pleasing to God and attain soul prosperity to be in health and also prosper financially and in all our ways.

Health

The unprospered soul somehow works against himself both in drawing negativity to himself and/or perpetuating ancestral issues in his bloodline. You've known of families that multiple members have the same disease, succumb to the same sicknesses, or die at similar ages. Sometimes it is a self-fulfilling prophecy, but sometimes it is not. A child may not know his biological parents but still suffer from the same health conditions that they did. That's because of ancestral altars. Without God and without repentance and prayer, some things will not, and cannot be stopped.

Unprospered emotions can lead to health problems by promoting emotional eating, for example. Binge eating. Not eating at all, due to the state of one's emotions. Bulimia and anorexia is bought on by people who do not have a healthy body image and they take things into their own hands and take things overboard. When we have our minds focused on Christ we can achieve balance, moderation, health, and healing in our physical bodies and in our emotions.

Emotions can also affect the flesh. Survival mode releases a storm of hormones in the body that make people unwell, sick, diseased. Sometimes dead. Survival emotions affect all systems of the body from the head to the muscles to the GI tract to the heart, to name a few. Survival mode is the body's reaction to save our lives, but we should not live there, perpetually.

Emotional drinking, drug abuse, as a result of emotions, from peer pressure, or any stress is a reality. Without the emotional control in our prospered souls and the Grace of God, any person might fall into the devil's traps.

Soul impulses are so strong that the person having the emotions, for example, can move their flesh and even make it unwell.

They say that the part of the body that you use to sin with is the part that gives the devil an open door to attack. Honestly look at your own sins and see if any health issue in your life correlates to how you (or your ancestors) sinned and what doors may have been opened for the enemy to work against you.

Salvation is the first step, but that is not all. Do not deceive yourself that all you need is Salvation and Jesus will do all the rest. Deliverance is needed. Your new car comes detailed from the dealer, but don't you wash it again every week or so?

Deliverance of the mind (soul) will bring prosperity of all kinds. **Spiritual prosperity is the key to all other kinds of prosperity.** Intellectual prosperity (education), physical prosperity is what is evident to other humans when you are looking good in the community and the world.

Sin with your soul, and your soul can come under attack. Soul sins? Unforgiveness. Bitterness. Resentment, and hatred, to name a few. **These are called works of the flesh because the flesh is most likely directing the soul to conduct these sins.**

Sin with your body--, sex sins, stealing, killing... your body can come under attack, outside of repentance and the Mercy of God.

Where is Your Money?

Prosperity is more than money, but it is money. Money answers all things (Eccl 10:19). Sins of money or sin with your money, with permission of your soul (***will***) and intellect, means you are aware that you are doing it, you did it on purpose. It is not a simple math error, these are sins.

We've spoken a great deal about the emotions, but the ***will*** and the intellect are part of the soul as well. When it comes to giving money and things, emotions can play a huge part, but the ***will*** steps up to facilitate or inhibit *giving*.

Freely give, freely receive. Give freely you will receive freely, that's what the Word says. Anytime you don't do what the Word says, you sin. Even if you don't KNOW what the Word says you are still responsible for knowing it if you are saved and of at least the age of accountability.

It is said that a person experiences real emotional pain when they let go of money. Of course, that depends on their relationship with money. Is money an idol to you? If it is, it surely will be very difficult to let go of it, even to pay your bills. No unsaved someone wants to part with their *idol*. Laban came running after Rachel to get the idols of his house when Rachel and Jacob finally left after 14 years, and she took those idols.

Jacob had another wife, Leah, two handmaids, 10 children, and Rachel, his favorite wife. Rachel took those idols from her dad's house when they left; Laban came to get them. He didn't have a problem so much with 2 daughters and 10 grandchildren leaving, but his idols are what he ran after.

Can't let go of money? If it's an idol to you, you will run after it and cling to it.

- Lord, show me if I am clinging on to money to my own soul's detriment, in Jesus' Name.

When emotions are running your spiritual life, a person may tithe sometimes or never. Offerings--, probably not. I was invited to a big church meeting by an extremely well-off male friend, his financial reputation preceded him; he was loaded. This man made it a point to find out where a certain popular, internationally known minister was speaking and asked me to go with him. I was kind of impressed thinking, *Wow, he's <u>saved</u> too? This is great!*

We got there in plenty of time to get a good seat. During the meeting this friend appeared to be listening to the speaker, and I thought this must be a testament to how God blesses *His* people! But when the offering basket was passed, this rich man refused to put in any money whatsoever. The basket came to me first and I was to pass it to him. I held it for what seemed like a *long* time, and he didn't budge to put anything in. This was especially noticeable because he had gotten two offering envelopes when we first sat down and had handed me one and kept one for himself.

I gave in the offering because I thought the message was good and the workman is worthy of honor, perhaps even double honor. As soon as the basket went past him and he put nothing in, I asked this wealthy man right then and there, why didn't he give in the offering? He said, *"That preacher is probably worth $ _____ (so many million dollars). He has more money than I do, he doesn't need my money."*

Whoa! Jealous much? Jealous of something that you don't even **know**, you just *think* you know it. My impression of him changed immediately. That's a man whose *soul* is running his life to some degree, and his spiritual life is probably a soulish life and not spiritual at all. At least God didn't seem to be in it.

The rich man disrespected the minister, in my opinion, he disrespected the ministry, the Church, the Word, disobeyed God and still has absolutely no way to take any of that money with him to Heaven or Hell.

Hell has hell's fire.

Heaven has the fire that will try a man's works. Hay, wood and stubble will burn. What will your works be to God? Will your works be more than hay, wood, or stubble? Only **gold** that has been tried in fire will not burn. An unprospered soul either doesn't know that or doesn't care.

A year later that man was facing one of those fires because a year later, that man was dead.

God Will Show Up

Soul prosperity, that's how you prosper because ***God will show up where you are***. Soul prosperity is how you behave when things aren't *yet* the way you want them, or the way God says they should be. Still, you seek God, and He shows up. By behaving in a mature, Christian way, you show God that you are trustworthy and that you are *able* to receive those things, **and** still conduct your life in a way that is appropriate before other saints and sinners.

God will not let you embarrass Him. But, because of your proper responses to life and in life, things you need or want will manifest in your life.

The blessings of the LORD are *Yea* and *Amen*. The blessings of the Lord make one rich and God adds no sorrow with them. God will keep you in perfect peace. He will not allow your soul to be in hell, or stay in hell, captive if you are seeking

Him and seeking soul prosperity. He shows up for you, revealing Himself to you.

When God shows up, He's got everything you need. He's got health and wealth, all things that every living person wants and needs to have the abundant life that Jesus came and died for us to have. He's coming to the soul that's prospered or at least trying--, maturing, perfecting, prospering, so go ahead and be *mature, (Evangelist Sally Lee).*

If your own child called with a need or in a crisis, there is not one good parent who wouldn't try to move Heaven and Earth to get to their child and they will bring things with them that the child did not even ask for. Band-aids, soup, drinks, blankets, prayers, money, cookies… you name it. God is like that. God is even **more** like that. We get that behavior from GOD.

Good kid or bad kid, parents will treat any of their children well over and over unless they finally realize that a bad kid will never change, or that that bad kid is using them or wasting their time, energy and money. It usually takes a long time though because that is *their* child.

God treats us even better than that, and He's got even more patience than that. But He says in His Word that He will not always strive with man. God will turn unrepentant people over to a reprobate mind, but for the most part He is patient.

Where's Your Money?

So, **where's your money?** The devil's got it? How did he get it? Is it being withheld from you in the heavenlies because you didn't pray your angels *through*?

Are you a captured soul? How did your soul become captive? How did the devil capture you? Sin. You or down your bloodline. Have you repented? Have you repented down your family bloodline yet? This is how you get out of captivity. This is how you prosper your soul. This is how you get all the stuff that the devil took from you. This is how you live a proper life, a life that honors God, not in survival mode. This is how you prosper your family, your bloodline, so your children and *children's* children will be further ahead in life than you were when you started out and even now. Repent, so God can be pleased with your bloodline, seeing that you are prospering.

(As an aside: Parents that's what's wrong with your kids, their little souls are *unprospered* when they think they know more than you and are *ahead* of you. They are *supposed* to be ahead of you, but they are unprospered in their souls, so it goes to their heads.)

You want that money; you want healing and health from God? **<u>First go get your soul</u>**. You may have to go get all the parts, pieces, and fragments that you have chipped away, that you've allowed to be chipped away, that you've been tricked out of. Go get all the parts that you've allowed to be stolen from you, held captive and tormented by the enemy of your soul, the enemy of God.

It says in Leviticus that the people would become *scattered* because of rejecting God, rejecting God's covenants, rejecting God's ways--, basically *sinning.* **That is true collectively and individually** *scattered*. Parts of your soul could be scattered. Parts of your soul could be in hell.

Parts of it could be scattered all over the community if you are soul tied. You fragmented your own soul if you allowed yourself to be soul-tied. It's in the house with your Ex, in the streets, across the state, the world; a part or parts of your soul could be in the place where you had the most fun you ever had in your life. It was SIN, but you want to do it again. You're Soul-tied.

I was recently receiving deliverance; the Lord gave me such peace. Peace that defied understanding, peace like a river. I felt whole, complete, I felt *gathered.* **Gathered**.

Jerusalem, Jerusalem, you who kill the prophets and stone those sent to you, **how often I have longed to gather your children together, as a hen gathers her chicks under her wings,** and you were not willing.

Matthew 23:37 NIV

I must ask you today, are you willing?

Are you willing to stop sinning? Are you willing to accept Truth? Are you willing to receive deliverance? Are you willing to show yourself approved? Are you willing to humble yourselves and pray, turn from your wicked ways the ways of your own understanding? Are you willing to be *gathered*, put back together, *re*membered, rather than scattered here there and everywhere? And captive?

That's where your health is; that's where your wealth and your money are, that's where your prosperity is. The prosperity of your body, your physical health, your emotional and mental health, all the parts of your mind are in your soul's prosperity. That is also where your money and your health are; it is all with your prospered soul.

Prospering

A prospered soul is devil-proof. An unprospered soul is the devil's food. We may think the unprospered soul flies off the handle at the drop of a hat; it does, but a soul can be unprospered in many other ways other than emotions. There is willful disobedience, rebellion, idolatry, and witchcraft, so a person can be unprospered in their *will*.

Any person who is supposed be at least at the age of maturity but is still behaving as a child would is not prospered in their soul; they haven't grown, they haven't matured. They haven't seen the big picture or recognized that Eternity needs to be factored into their daily decisions and behaviors.

The unprospered soul is very now-minded as survival mode is now-minded.

One of the main things that would hinder a soul from prospering is survival *memory*. Another thing is sitting in the seat of the scornful--, listening to a liar or a *lying spirit*, not being grounded but tossed about by winds of doctrine.

A faithless man is unprospered in his soul. A man with no Fruit of the Spirit on board is unprospered, as is a man who walks by the flesh, walks by sight and not by faith, as is the prideful man, the ungrateful, and the entitled.

On the other end of the spectrum, an insecure, doubting, uncertain, depressed, man who is poor in spirit but is not seeking God and has no idea who he is will not be prospered in his soul.

Any false balance of identity is indicative of an unprospered soul.

A man with an unrenewed mind even if he tries to prosper in his soul, his old way of thinking will interfere with every stride his soul will try to make.

Soul-Tied

The soul tied man cannot prosper his soul because it is tied to another's soul, or he is in the wrong realm, timeline or dimension. What? IKR. A captive soul can be in another whole realm.

If you had a beautiful horse, for example, rode it into town and tied it to the hitching post, or wherever people tie their horses and then you caught the stagecoach to the next town; how will you *minister* to your horse that is tied in the previous town? How will you feed it, groom it, nurture it or even give it drink? It is tied in another *realm*. Let's say it's the realm of Dodge City and there you are in Cheyenne.

Well, one can tie their soul or allow their soul to be tied to another person, thing, time of life, and it precludes the growth of that soul. It stops the maturing of that soul. It will hinder any kind of progress that soul can make because of being ***tied***.

It's like time travel except there is no travel you are stuck in the same place. So, it's more like Ground Hog Day (the movie) or all the movies where people keep repeating the same day over and again. At least in the cinema world once the person "gets it right" they can escape out of the time vortex, realm, or dimension. But with the soul tie you repeat the same thing, the same day, the same hurt, the same sin (virtually) or whatever you are repeating over and over again, *ad nauseum*.

How?

Mentally. Virtually.

In your mind you are asking yourself, *Why did this happen, How did this happen? Why doesn't he love me anymore?* Or you are remembering when it was so wonderful or so terrible between you and the object of your relationship desires, or hatred. You are stuck in time. Ground Hog Day.

Being stuck there you are not ministering to your soul, you are not feeding it, you are not growing, maturing or prospering your soul leads to arrested development. Your flesh might be getting older, but you are ***willing*** yourself to stay the same, the last time the two of you were together, or were happy together. **You are willing yourself to NOT prosper in your emotions, in your soul.**

A soul-tied person has allowed their soul to be fragmented and the part that is stuck is not prospering. When you prosper in your soul, you need to prosper your _whole_ soul, not just a part of it.

The thing that is tying the soul-tied person down is their own memory, which can be real or fantasized. It can be realistic or romanticized. What happened may not have even happened at all or happened the way the person has "remembered" it.

Don't deceive yourself. This whole thing is a problem.

Encourage Yourself in The Lord

I discussed in **Souls in Captivity** how to get out of captivity and how to stop being an unprospered soul due to memories that could tie a person down. These are the steps:

- Know your emotions.
- Own your emotions.
- Manage your emotions.
- Encourage yourself.

David encouraged himself in the Lord. At Ziklag in the OT, David had lost everything, including his family. The memories of that could have tied David down for a long time or forever. David had to rise above his own *memories* of seeing the destruction and losses of Ziklag, there were probably dead bodies strewn about; that can be a debilitating memory. David had to encourage himself in the Lord, else how could he have gone forward? An unprospered soul would have bolted him down to the Earth and he could have sat there until he died. Or he could have retreated completely, never fighting for what he should have been fighting for.

Don't let an unprospered soul sit you down, bolt you down or cause you to retreat when you should be advancing! No matter what the memory, don't let it tie you down, tie you up, capture you in a net, or entangle your destiny.

When the devil puts his evil spin on your memories, the same memories that God gave us to **save** our lives, you must resist that devil, and encourage yourself like David did.

Learn to encourage yourself. Know what God says about you, and not what others are saying. Learn to encourage yourself. *Hey, I am the righteousness of God in Christ Jesus. I am blessed coming in and blessed going out. Yeah. I'm going to go out just to be going out to see if I'm blessed, then I'm going to come back in because God said it's so, it must be so. Thank you, Jesus.*

Like David, I am a mighty warrior, the Lord is with me in every battle, and we will not be defeated. We will recover all!

You're a Role Model

As you know, people are watching us Christians, all the time--, saved and unsaved. As they are watching you, you must exhibit soul prosperity. You can make godly choices, godly decisions, take godly actions, and have godly responses when your soul is in order.

> Beloved, I wish above all things you may prosper and be in health even as your soul prospers. 3 John 2

When the soul is well ordered, all types of prosperity--, health, financial, emotional, intellectual, and spiritual prosperity will flow automatically, according to your faith. The reason we want soul prosperity is not to have *things and stuff*. But, with soul prosperity, we automatically get blessings from God. You automatically get *things and stuff*.

Yes, we all can have emotions and moods, but a prospered soul can find his *center* again quickly. A prospered soul, even when under attack, or going *through*, can find GOD again very quickly, immediately.

A prospered soul does not need to vent to every friend and fake friend because a prospered soul knows how to encourage *himself* in the LORD because his mind is stayed on God. So when that prospered soul is going through, he or she will immediately and always PRAY.

Whether or not we have our minds stayed on the Lord will be told in the outcomes of our decisions.

AMEN.

Prayer

We thank You, Lord, for the Word that tells us we are to prosper and be in health as our soul prospers and for our emotions. Lord, we ask you to touch emotions today. We ask you to touch emotion so that we all can know that we do not have to respond or react out of our emotions, but we have a rational brain. We have a renewed mind because we are new creations in Christ. We have the ability to prosper, and long as we do, You will prosper us in the things of health and even material things. And Lord, we don't seek after those things. We will seek after soul prosperity.

Thank You, Lord. That in our memories and our imprints we have a God-focused view and that even the ones that we had before you Lord, as they come by the washing of the water of the Word, wash us anew that we are able to forgive people, forgive hurts and put perspective on things and forget those things that are behind and press forward. We thank

You, Lord, that we can have soul prosperity, so we can navigate in this life, make right decisions, treat others well, as the Word says. So that the Mind of Christ will be in us because we will be doing as Jesus would do.

It's all to the praise of your glory. But we thank You today, and we honor You. We love You, Lord, and we bless You for all the blessings of 3 John 2, in the Name of Jesus.

Amen.

Christian books by this author

AK: Adventures of the Agape Kid

AMONG SOME THIEVES

As My Soul Prospers

Behave

Bitterness & Unforgiveness: Devil Weapons

Churchzilla (The Wanna-Be Bride of Christ)

The Coco-So-So Correct Show

Demons Hate Questions

Do Not Orphan Your Seed

Do Not Work for Money

Don't Refuse Me Lord

Fantasy Spirit Spouse

The FAT Demons

got Money?

Let Me Have a Dollar's Worth

Living for the NOW of God

Lord, Help My Debt

Lose My Location

Made Perfect In Love

The Man Safari *(Really, I'm Just Looking)*

Marriage Ed., *Rules of Engagement & Marriage*

The Motherboard: *Key to Soul Prosperity*

My Life As A Slave

Name Your Seed

Plantation Souls

The Poor Attitudes of Money

Power Money: Nine Times the Tithe

The Power of Wealth

Seasons of Grief

Seasons of War

SOULS in Captivity

Soul Prosperity: *Your Health & Your Wealth*

The *spirit* of Poverty

The Throne of Grace, *Courtroom Prayers*

Upgrade: How to Get Out of Survival Mode

Warfare Prayer Against Poverty

When the Devourer is Rebuked

The Wilderness Romance

Other Journals & Devotionals by this author:

The Cool of the Day – Journal for times spent with God

got HEALING? Verses for Life

got HOPE? Verses for Life

got WISDOM? Verses for Life

got GRACE? Verses for Life

got JOY? Verses for Life

got PEACE? Verses for Life

got LOVE? Verses for Life

He Hears Us, Prayer Journal *in 4 different colors*

I Have A Star, Dream Journal *in styles for kids, teen, young adult and up.*

I Have A Star, Guided Prayer Journal, *2 styles: Boy or Girl*

J'ai une Etoile, Journal des Reves

Let Her Dream, Dream Journal *in multiple colors*

Men Shall Dream, Dream Journal, *(blue or black)*

My Favorite Prayers *(in 4 styles)*

My Sowing Journal *(in three different colors)*

Tengo una Estrella, Diario de Sueños

Wise Counsel Journal

Illustrated children's books by this author:

Big Dog (8-book series)

Do Not Say That to Me

Every Apple

Fluff the Clouds

I Love You All Over the World

Imma Dance

The Jump Rope

Kiss the Sun

The Masked Man

Not During a Pandemic

Push the Wind

Tangled Taffy

What If?

Wiggle, Wiggle; Giggle, Giggle

Worry About Yourself

You Did Not Say Goodbye to Me

www.ingramcontent.com/pod-product-compliance
Lightning Source LLC
Chambersburg PA
CBHW062119080426
42734CB00012B/2913